AMBETH R. OCAMPO has, for over three decades, brought history down from academia and returned it to the public where it also belongs. Drawing from extensive archival research, at home and abroad, he has written on Philippine history focusing on its art, culture, and the heroes who figure in the birth of the nation.

Dr. Ocampo is an associate professor and former chair, Department of History, Ateneo de Manila University. He writes a widely read editorial page column for the *Philippine Daily Inquirer*, moderates a growing Facebook fan page, and also connects on Instagram. An independent curator, he sits on the advisory boards of the Ateneo Art Gallery, Ayala Museum, BenCab Museum, Lopez Museum, and the President Elpidio Quirino Foundation.

In other lives and other times he was a Benedictine monk; president of the City College of Manila; chairman, National Historical Commission of the Philippines and the National Commission on Culture and the Arts; chairman, Incoming State Visits, Office of Presidential Protocol, Malacañang Palace; and adviser, Numismatic Committee, Bangko Sentral ng Pilipinas. After an eventful professional and personal life, he looks forward to the perks of a senior citizen card.

Other books by *AMBETH* R. OCAMPO:

The Paintings of E. Aguilar Cruz (1986)
Rizal Without the Overcoat rev. ed. (2011)
Makamisa: The Search for Rizal's Third Novel rev. ed. (2009)
A Calendar of Rizaliana in the Vault of the Philippine National Library rev. ed. (2011)
Aguinaldo's Breakfast (1993)
Bonifacio's Bolo (1995)
Mabini's Ghost (1995)
Teodora Alonso (1995)
Talking History: Conversations with Teodoro A. Agoncillo rev. ed. (2011)
Luna's Moustache (1997)
The Centennial Countdown (1998)
Bones of Contention rev. ed. (2014)
Meaning and History: The Rizal Lectures rev. ed. (2013)
101 Stories of the Philippine Revolution (2009)
Looking Back rev. ed. (2009)
Looking Back 2: Dirty Dancing (2010)
Looking Back 3: Death by Garrote rev. ed. (2015)
Looking Back 4: Chulalongkorn's Elephants rev. ed. (2016)
Looking Back 5: Rizal's Teeth, Bonifacio's Bones (2012)
Looking Back 6: Prehistoric Philippines (2012)
Looking Back 7: Storm Chasers (2014)
Looking Back 8: Virgin of Balintawak (2014)
Looking Back 9: Demonyo Tables (2015)
Looking Back 10: Two Lunas, Two Mabinis (2015)
Looking Back 11: Independence x6 (2016)
Looking Back 12: Quezon's Sukiyaki (2017)

Guns of the Katipunan

Looking Back 13

Ambeth R. Ocampo

Looking Back 13
Guns of the Katipunan

Philippine Copyright © Ambeth R. Ocampo, 2017

Published and exclusively distributed by
ANVIL PUBLISHING, INC.
7th Floor Quad Alpha Centrum
125 Pioneer Street, Mandaluyong City
1550 Philippines
Trunk lines: (+632) 8477-4752, 8477-4755 to 57
Fax: (+632) 8747-1622,
sales@anvilpublishing.com,
onlinesales@anvilpublishing.com,
marketing@anvilpublishing.com,
www.anvilpublishing.com

First printing, 2017
Second printing, 2018
Third printing, 2020

Cover design by R. Jordan P. Santos
Copyedited by Renán S. Prado

ISBN 978-621-420-214-0

Printed in the Philippines

Contents

Preface

Preface

Textbook history give us the outcome of battles, but rarely provides the details: how these battles were fought, what weapons were used, what kind of damage or wounds certain weapons would inflict on the combatants, etc. In the 1980's, rummaging through all the assorted odds and ends collected by Mario Alcantara at Heritage Art Center in Quezon City, I found a flyer with a short Tagalog poem written by a young lady from San Roque, Cavite in 1898 that described first-hand the war waged by Emilio Aguinaldo against the Spaniards. She said the gunfire during battle resembled the terrible rumble of thunder, yet through all the noise she could distinguish the sound made by particular guns:

> "...palconete't cañon Revolver, Remington ang putoc bung bung
> ang Mauser at Riple ay pac bung pac bung."

Palconete, cannon, Revolver and Remington go "bung-bung" Mauser and Rifle go "pac bung pac bung" this simple poem, ignored by most historians focused on the great narrative, inspired me to see into the forest and look at the trees. Friends described this attention to detail as "micro-history" while critics labeled it "trivia" or sometimes "chismis." God, they say, is in the details, and if it these can add color and understanding to the sepia-toned history we were forced to learn in school then the effort to dig them up and deploy them in my writing has been worthwhile.

Ambeth R. Ocampo
11 July 2017 Feast of St. Benedict of Nursia.

Guns of the Katipunan

OF the handful of books that contain a transcript of the trial of Andres Bonifacio, the most useful is the one edited by Miguel Bernad, S. J., and published by the Ateneo in 1963. This edition contains an offset reprint of the original Tagalog documents. Often overlooked in the Bonifacio trial is a seemingly boring inventory of arms made on April 29, 1897, by Lazaro Makapagal. Trivial is the word used to describe this list of guns, but these were the arms confiscated from Bonifacio and his companions when he was arrested in Limbon.

Confronted with this list, one looks in vain for Bonifacio's famous bolo. In the absence of a bolo, one asks which of those guns must have been Bonifacio's personal weapon. Bonifacio was charged with shooting at the arresting party that claimed self-defense to explain the encounter that led to the death of Ciriaco Bonifacio. To counter this assertion, Bonifacio requested that his guns be produced and examined since they would have full barrels that prove he had not fired a single shot. Naturally, this was not acted on. Bonifacio was found guilty, and the rest is history.

There were two Mausers in the list, one with number L 2798 plate bearing the initials A.B. (in the original Tagalog *katkat ang plancha at may tandang A.B.*) Did this signify Andres Bonifacio, or *Anak ng Bayan*? Could these be the initials of the gun dealer or the manufacturer?

The other was a Mauser K 2894 with additional No. 1 plate bearing the initials A.B. In the original manuscript the A.B. can also be read as H.B. What did these initials mean? Could H.B. mean *Haring Bayan* or "Sovereign People," a title Bonifacio took and which his critics claimed actually meant *Hari ng Bayan* or "King of the People"? Maybe the initials could also be *Hukbong Bayan* or Armed Forces? From these entries alone, one can demonstrate how much two letters or the spacing between letters can mean to a student of history.

Aside from the two Mausers listed there are: fourteen Remingtons; one shotgun (*escupeta*) with double barrel; one shotgun (*escupeta de un kañon de piston*); three (single barrel?) shotguns with central fire (*escupeta de fuego central*); two shotguns with double barrel; one shotgun, Saun(?); and (four *Arabucos* or *Trabucos*, translated as Blunderbusses, one with the markings "Juan Estrella."

Textbooks narrate the events of the Philippine

KUNDIMAN

Buhat nğ ma-usong damit na cundiman
sa mğa binatang binaro't salaual
quinorpiño naman nang cadalagahan
siyang pag sang-almas nang catagalugan.

Uicang Kalayaa'y dito pinag gamit
at ang Katipunan sa pagca capatid
tatlong letrang **K** umiral guinamit
sa sulat tagalog ang C inaligpit.

At cung nangdidigmá ang mğa tagalog
ang dalang sandata'y mahahabang guloc
sibat na búcaue pinag lulumagot
may bárol, may puñal, sump't at arcabus.

Trencilla sa bilog mulá nang umiral
ang mğa dalaga'y nag iba nang asal
ang utos castila ay niyuyuracan
mag sariling camot laguing gunamgunam.

Dito na dumatal caramihang vapor
ang dalang sandata palconete't cañon
Revolver, Remington ang putóc bung bung
ang Mauser at Riple ay pac bung pac bung.

At cun rumapido'y caquila-quilabot
dinaig pa yata elementong culog.
lupa'y yumayanig sa saliu nang putóc
bala'y nag halinghing niyong pananalot.

Ang mğa kastila'y cun uma-abance
sasacay sa vapor at cacañong mabute
uala mang maquíta na tauo sa tabi
nagpapaputóc di't tacot ay malaqui.

Capitan Emilio hindi natatacot
sa bala nang cañon halos ganga palioc
pananalig niya'y malaqui sa Dios
at sa pintacasi Magdalenang bantog.

Quinatha nang isang dalaga na taga San Roque---Kavite. 1898.

Pamphlet with an 1898 poem by a young lady from San Roque, Cavite
that details the sounds different types of guns make.

revolution against Spain and the Filipino-American War but rarely give a clear picture of how the war was fought. What kind of weapons did the Filipinos use? What are Mausers? Remingtons? Krags? The picture book *The War in the Philippines*, written by an enemy captain Harry Wells, gives us descriptions of the war that accompany the pictures. Although the book's subject is the Filipino-American War, the weapons used were of the same type as those used by Bonifacio and the Katipunan during the revolution.

According to Wells, the Mauser rifle with which the Spanish Army is armed and which constitutes the majority of the arms of the Filipinos, is a magazine gun holding five shells and having a caliber of .27 3-10, being even smaller than the .30 caliber Krag-Jorgensen rifle used by our regular army. Its range is somewhat longer than that of the Krag-Jorgensen, and much longer than the .45 caliber Springfield with which the volunteers are armed.

To the general reader the above is unintelligible. Fortunately, Wells provides something more graphic:

The Mauser bullet is a small piece of lead encased in a steel jacket, which renders it very hard and enables it to pierce hard substances without being battered out of shape. It makes a round, smooth hole, even through bones, and does not mangle the flesh and break the bones like the larger, soft Springfield bullets. Thus the amputation of an arm or of a leg because of a wound from a Mauser is very rare, while the wounds from Springfield bullets render such amputation frequently necessary.

On the other hand, the Remingtons were:

...of the same caliber as the Springfield, No. 45. The cartridge is a pointed lead slug encased in a brass jacket. Wounds from these brass-covered bullet were apt to be poisoned by verdigris, and several cases of that kind occurred. If the brass casing was split when the bullet was fired, the jagged ends made a horrible noise going through the air. A volunteer protested that the Filipinos were firing sewing machines and tin cans at him, and I heard one man say that these split brass bullets had whiskers and saw teeth.

Critics say details like these are useless trivia, *tsismis* at best. However, without details we can never paint a human face on history.

Shortage of bullets
bugged Katipuneros

ONE of the defects of textbook history is the lack of details regarding the way the Philippine revolution against Spain and the Filipino-American War was fought. We are not told, for example, that Filipinos were poorly armed. Whatever guns they had on hand were picked up from the enemy either in battle or through what we would call today *agaw-armas*. The bigger problem was that even if they had guns, they did not have sufficient ammunition. This explains the numerous orders, sometimes even to children, to return to a battle site and gather empty cartridges.

Daniel Tirona, alias "Nahahanda," writing from Haligui on February 5, 1897, explained:

> Considering our dire need for Remington bullets, and the great shortage that this Army has for cartridges, I beg your Honors [the Presidents

of towns] to order our soldiers to pick up empty shells in a place where a battle has taken place. If any are found, please send them at once to headquarters. I hope earnestly that you will do this, for in our sacred cause of freedom, we must help each other for the common good.

Tactics changed little whether the Filipinos were fighting Spaniards from 1896 to 1898 or Americans from 1899 onwards. There was always the lack of bullets and the need to reload spent or used cartridges. An American soldier remarked:

> When the Filipinos ran short of ammunition for their Remingtons they saved the shells as they fired them and took them back to be reloaded. I have seen a whole sackful of these empty shells captured and a great many of their reloaded cartridges. They also bought the empty shells of our own Springfields from Chinamen, which our authorities negligently permitted them to gather up after a battle. I have seen hundreds of these reloaded Springfield shells and have several in my possession. Their crude workmanship and the brand of our own manufacturers in the end easily identify them.

Perhaps someone will argue that the above is a biased enemy account. But even our own General Jose Alejandrino in his memoirs writes:

It could hardly be said that there was a military administration. The few arsenals which we had were poorly equipped; their principal work was to refill the empty cartridges. In these conditions, we took for granted beforehand that it would be impossible for us to sustain a determined attack of the enemy for more than 24 hours. The difficulties increased when we take into account the different makes and calibers of our armaments. In fact, it was found that to a regiment were being sent ammunition which could not be utilized because they were of a make and caliber different from those of their guns. This produced very harmful delays and confusion in the campaigns.

Empty cartridges were reloaded in the same way that we would reink old printer ribbons today. In the prehistoric days of dot-matrix printers, people would scrimp on expensive "original" ribbons and reink the ribbons. When this proved too messy some went to computer stores and paid someone to reload the original cartridges with generic ribbon not of the manufacturer's own make. The analogy is not quite exact, but it brings the Katipuneros closer to our experience and imagination.

Katipuneros reloaded empty cases with crude homemade gunpowder made from saltpeter or *salitre* (the main ingredient for pork *tocino*) mixed with ground

Filipino soldiers in formation showing their guns and uniforms

charcoal and sulphur. The Katipuneros used primitive primers and of course had no way of knowing the exact proportions to make good gunpowder. Neither did they have the right recipe for the mixture of gunpowder and the lead they beat into bullets. Naturally, some of these crude reloaded bullets exploded in their guns and injured the Filipinos rather than the enemy. Jammed guns were the least damage these reloaded cartridges caused.

If there was a shortage of bullets, it follows that the Filipinos did not have shooting practice. At one point Aguinaldo ordered his men not to waste bullets and to hold their fire until the enemy was about twenty feet away. How adept were the Filipinos with guns? In general orders to the military issued from Malolos in March 1899, Aguinaldo wrote:

> It is being noted that one of the defects in our soldiers is that of aiming too high...officers shall constantly direct all to correct this fault, and endeavor to shoot rather too low than too high, as a low aim gives better results than a high one. The troops should be reminded that the favorable result of a battle does not depend upon a large number of shots being fired, but on good firing; and that a good shot is worth more than many without result, which would only encourage the enemy if he sees that they do not cause him a heavy loss.

We would like to believe that all the Katipuneros were marksmen, that all revolutionaries are brave. History makes us stop to smell the coffee (or the gunpowder) and realize that the revolution was fought by humans not invincible superheroes.

Courage was Filipinos' main weapon

EXTANT documents on the Philippine revolution prove that things were not as simple as they are made out to be in textbooks and movies. For example, the inventory sent to headquarters by the president of *Maypagibig* in December 1896 will make us realize that the real weapon in the revolution was not guns or bolos but raw courage. This group only had: "*16 ang binabalahat ng kapsula* (guns requiring cartridges); *2 escupetang dalawa ang kañon* (two double-barreled shotguns); *5 escupetang isang kañon ngune dalawa ang sira* (five single-barreled shotguns, but two are defective!); one rifle owned by Florencio Laviña."

This appears to be a trivia list unworthy of "serious academic" notice, but for the general reader, this inventory drives home the point that the Katipuneros fought with little else but bravery (or was it folly?) with few guns, fewer bullets, and no target practice, how did the Katipuneros feel on the battlefield? I doubt if their arms inspired any confidence in them at all.

Around the last quarter of 1896, the Katipuneros maintained a munitions plant in San Francisco de Malabon (now General Trias). It was run by Feliciano Jocson, a pharmacist from Manila known as "Totong" or "Patola." With a large quantity of saltpeter and his professional training, he supervised the Katipunan gunpowder factory.

Jose Ignacio Pawa, a Chinese blacksmith from Tondo who later rose in the ranks and became a general, set up another factory in Imus for the repair of guns and reloading of cartridges and muzzles. He also made bamboo cannons (probably the type we use at New Year) that was crudely reinforced with baling wire. Although these bamboo cannons were only effective at very close range, they boosted the morale of frontliners in a direct attack on the enemy. Despite their shortcomings, these bamboo cannons were a definite improvement from lances or bolos that were only useful at literally an arm's length from the enemy.

It appears that the industrious and creative General Pawa also made *paltiks*. The guns on display at the *Museo ng Rebolusyon* in Pinaglabanan look like ordinary metal tubes attached to triggers and handles. On January 14, 1897, a certain Modesto Dimla "Matianac" wrote to General Vito Belarmino offering a metal pipe he had bought to be converted into trabucos or blunderbusses. He even offered to cover all expenses provided the guns made out of his *tubo* are strong and sturdy. Today, one still sees these steel pipes under drivers' seats for use in traffic brawls. A century ago, these pieces of *tubo* were made into *paltiks*.

People imagine Katipuneros as always armed with bolos. But what about other indigenous weapons, like blowguns, darts, and bows and arrows? On December 16, 1896, Baldomero Aguinaldo alias "Mabangis" wrote to the presidents of Cavite towns saying:

> It had been noted that there has been a great laxity in implementing orders issued by this Government of the 12th of last month, concerning the usefulness of the bow-and-arrow as a weapon against the enemy in battle...I should explain that, for best results the bow should be as tall as the user, and that the quiver should contain thirty arrows. In addition, the traditional bolo (*gulok*) or dagger (*puñal*) should be worn at the waist. This order affects all males from eighteen years old or over. Exempted are the soldiers equipped with guns, and old people. The aforementioned weapons should be constantly carried about.

From all the foreign films we have seen from childhood, it appears that the bow and arrow was useful to Robin Hood in medieval Nottingham and to Indians in the wild American west. But was it to be used in the late nineteenth-century Cavite? Against Spaniards, and later against Americans? Most Caviteños did not think this a bright idea and ignored Baldomero Aguinaldo's instructions, prompting him to reiterate on January 16, 1897:

> Up to now, many have complied with the order that all males from fifteen to fifty [years of age] should have their own bow and arrows. Each quiver should have a minimum of thirty arrows, the more the better...All males...comply within five days from the time this order is announced... Do not let laziness stand in the way: this bad habit should be done away with.

It is difficult to imagine Bonifacio or Aguinaldo with a bow and arrow, but in war the Filipinos used all manner of weapons and all types of warfare. Research into the weapons of the revolution will prove that real history is not as simple as textbook history.

Filipino soldiers at ease.

Filipinos never a factor in talks

HOSTILITIES in the Spanish-American War should have stopped upon the signing of a peace protocol in Washington on August 12, 1898. History, however, is filled with unexpected twists. On the next day, August 13, 1898, Spanish Manila fell to the Americans and the Stars and Stripes flew over Intramuros. News of the peace protocol had not reached the American naval and military forces before the attack because of the time difference between Manila and Washington. Communication by cable was not direct from Manila to the rest of the world.

One issue later debated on the bargaining table in Paris between the Spanish and American peace commissioners concerned "the control, disposition, and government of the Philippines." Spain insisted on the peace protocol signed on August 12 and demanded the return of Manila by right of conquest and would occupy and hold the city, bay, and harbor of Manila pending the conclusions of the Treaty of Peace in Paris. Spain later asked that Manila be returned pending the conclusion of the Treaty of Paris. Naturally, the United States refused.

Before the American commissioners left for Paris in September 1898, they were briefed in the White House by President McKinley who gave his position on the Philippines. Whitelaw Reid records the conclusion of this White House briefing in this journal:

> The President then remarked that he believed the acquisition of territory was naturally attractive to the American mind...but thought it would probably be more attractive just now than later on, when the difficulties, expense and loss of life which it entailed, became more manifest. He thought we could not possibly give up Manila, and doubted the wisdom of attempting to hold it without the entire island to which it belonged. Beyond this he did not seem inclined to go.
>
> He thereupon read the instructions which were explicit on other points, and indicated that he would fill out the gap with reference to the Philippines in the sense of the opinions he had just expressed. He closed the meeting after some remarks about the satisfaction he had in enlisting our services. [He desires] that we should use our best judgement on the Philippine question, and accumulate all possible information. [He

suggested] that, after hearing from Merritt and Dewey (to the opinion of the latter of whom be seemed to attach great importance), we might find it necessary for the safety of Luzon to provide also for acquiring some of the smaller islands near it.

McKinley's position as of September 13, 1898, was only to take Luzon, pending the opinion of Dewey that for him carried the most weight. By October 20, 1898, McKinley cabled instructions to the peace commissioners in Paris through the Secretary of State John Hay. McKinley had changed his mind and instructed the commissioners to demand the cession not only of Luzon but of the entire Philippine archipelago:

> While the Philippines can be justly claimed by conquest, which position must not be yielded, yet their disposition, control, and government the President prefers should be the subject of negotiation, as provided in the protocol. It is imperative upon us that as victors we should be governed only by motives which exalt our nation. Territorial expansion should be our last concern; that we shall not shirk the moral obligations of our victory is of the greatest [concern].
>
> It is undisputed that Spain's authority is permanently destroyed in every part of the Philippines. To leave any part in her feeble control now would increase our difficulties

and be opposed to the interests of humanity. The sentiment in the United States is almost universal that the people of the Philippines, whatever else is done, must be liberated from Spanish domination. In this sentiment the President fully concurs. Nor can we invite another power of powers to join the United States in governing them. We must either hold them or turn them back to Spain.

Consequently, grave as are the responsibilities and unforeseen as are the difficulties which are before us, the President can see but one path of duty—the acceptance of the archipelago....The terms upon which the full cession of the Philippines shall be made must be left largely with the Commission. But as its negotiations shall proceed it will develop the Spanish position, and if any new phase of the situation arises, the Commission can further communicate with the President. How these instructions shall be carried out....the President leaves to the judgment and discretion of the Commissioners.

Morality was used to cover up the issue of territorial expansion. For McKinley, returning the Philippines to Spain was "immoral." However, nowhere in McKinley's instructions do we Filipinos enter the picture.

Washington ignored
Filipino aspirations

THE skyline along Roxas Boulevard continues to change as every inch of space with a view of the postcard-pretty Manila Bay sunset is turned into commercial buildings or plush high-rise condominiums. Eventually, "development" will move inward and eat into the genteel district of Malate.

One of the casualties of land development might be a small house on 2200 M.H. del Pilar behind the present Hotel Sofitel (still called Silahis by many) where Felipe Agoncillo, the first Filipino diplomat, and his wife Marcela, who made the first Philippine flag in Hong Kong in 1898, used to live. Felipe died in 1941 and Marcela in 1946, but they continue to live even as names in textbook history. One of little-read documents of 1898 is the "Memorandum addressed by Felipe Agoncillo Minister Plenipotentiary of the Philippine Revolutionary Government to His Excellency William McKinley President of the United

States of North America concerning the situation and aspirations of the Filipino People October 3, 1898" written in Washington where he vainly worked for recognition of the First Philippine Republic. The memorandum is worth rereading today in the context of Spain's cession of the archipelago to the United States. Some of the points taken were:

1. Immediately after the Spanish War, the American representatives and officers in Singapore, Hong Kong, and Manila invited the natives of the Philippine Islands to second the action of the American armed forces which action they seconded with pleasure and loyalty, as allies, in the conviction that their personality and their political autonomous and sovereign rights would be recognized.

2. In order that such action be efficacious and executive it was necessary (a) to organize the army of the Philippines; (b) to organize their military staff and headquarters; and (c) to organize a government independent from America and Spain....

3. All this was done with the consent of the admiral in command of the fleet and of the generals and military political officers of the United States of America in the Philippine Islands, who aware of it, not only did not

object to it but accepted it as a consummated fact and maintained official relations with the new organization, utilizing the same for their subsequent activities and for carrying on the campaign which was consequently brought to a successful conclusion.

4. In the Protocol between the United States of America and Spain....both nations [were] to negotiate and conclude the Treaty of Peace in which it would be determined who was to control the Philippines, and what was to be the form of government.

5. Neither one State nor the other apparently gave attention to the right of the Filipinos to participate in this determination which will affect their destiny in history.

6. The Lawful government of the natives now functioning in the Philippine Islands has been sanctioned by the only legitimate authority and representation it has, and it has in fact been recognized, not objected to and utilized by the American nation...

7. The present lawful Philippine Government, of which the invincible leader General Emilio Aguinaldo is the President, also believes that the moment has come to remind and even to notify, if proper, in a formal and precise manner, the illustrious President and Government of

Washington of its existence and normal and regular functioning, as well as of its relations of reciprocity with the authorities of the American Republic in the Philippine Islands.

8. It desires to state (in the same manner), that the Filipino people unanimously confirm their independence and confide that the American people will recognize the same, mindful of the offers made and obligations contracted in its name, proclaiming the principles of liberty, justice, and right expressed in its famous, sacred Declaration of Independence for the benefit of the new nation which logically rises in that part of the globe under the impulse of its present beneficient and humanitarian action.

9. And the Filipino people hope that pending a permanent understanding for the evacuation of their territory their lawful *de facto* government will be accorded the rights of a belligerent...

10. The Filipino people and their aforesaid Government and legitimate representatives pray and urge the noble president of the United States of America and the Public powers thereof to be guided by the aspirations, recognize the rights, sanctions, and proclaim, imbued by their sentiments of justice, honor that which was offered by their international representatives, as set forth in this document.

All of Agoncillo's efforts were in vain. His memoranda and letters were ignored by the White House and the peace commission in Paris as the existence of a functioning Filipino government complicated the U.S. bid to take the Philippines from Spain.

U.S. political cartoon showing Uncle Sam's boot on the Philippines, ignoring Aguinaldo's sign to keep off.

US saw RP an ideal colony

HISTORIANS writing on the American intrusion into our history usually use a Senate document printed in 1899 entitled *Message from the President of the United States transmitting a Treaty of Peace between the United States and Spain*, signed at the city of Paris on December 10, 1898. Since the so-called Treaty of Paris required ratification by the U.S. Senate, papers were attached to the document to guide the senators in making their decision for or against the treaty. Negotiations between the U.S. and Spanish commissioners are given, as well as U.S. consular and military reports on Aguinaldo and the Philippines.

Aside from the Treaty of Paris and its accompanying papers, another source of information on the U.S. decision to take the Philippines is the diary of commissioner Whitelaw Reid. His pro-expansionist viewpoint gives us an idea of what the Americans saw in the Philippines.

During the White House briefing shortly before the peace commissioners left for Paris, Reid expressed these views:

> I spoke of the great importance of the Philippines with reference to trade in China, of the difficulty morally of taking one part and abandoning the rest to Spain, and of the political difficulties flowing from the same policy, which it seemed to me, would be merely organizing in a worse shape exactly the trouble we have been suffering from in the West Indies for the past three quarters of a century...I believed it too difficult to hold Manila alone without the island to which it belonged, or to hold any other harbor on Luzon. The hinterland seemed to be a necessity.

> I believed also that the commerce of the Philippines themselves with the United States would be very considerable. Our possession of them would give us an enormous advantage in the vastly greater commerce that might be cultivated in China. I believed their possession valuable to the country, but especially important to the Pacific Coast.

> We were at present at a disadvantage in commerce on the Atlantic Ocean, and could hardly expect in our time, or in that of the next generation, to catch up with Great Britain. We already had, however, an enormous advantage on

the Pacific Ocean. The acquisition of the Sandwich Islands [Hawaii] greatly strengthened us in this field. If to this we now added the Philippines, it would be possible for American energy to build up such a commercial marine on the Pacific Coast as should ultimately convert the Pacific Ocean into an American lake, making it far more our own than the Atlantic Ocean is now Great Britain's. Such a possession therefore would tend to stimulate our shipbuilding industry and commerce, and could not but add immensely to the national prosperity.

I strongly deprecated the idea of making two bites of the cherry. I was not so much concerned about whether it would be immediately popular or not, though on this point I had little doubt of the popular tendency. What concerned me more was whether it should be left to the people of a succeeding generation to dwell on the magnificent opportunities that Providence had thrown in our way, and to record that the men in charge of public affairs at the time were unable to comprehend or grasp their opportunities, and had thus thrown away the magnificent future that should have belonged to the nation.

....Our true national interest, therefore, was to seek a development for our commerce particularly with countries who needed what we had to sell and could not produce, and who could offer us in exchange what we needed and could not produce. The Philippines seemed to me to meet these conditions; so did China. The control of the Pacific Ocean pointed almost exclusively to a commerce under these conditions and seemed to me therefore to offer the largest and best commercial future of the country.

The suggestion that we should take any part of the Philippines as a war indemnity, though plausible, seemed to me unnecessary. We had taken the capital of the country, the center of its administration, the point from which it was controlled. In doing so we had taken prisoner practically the whole Spanish army of occupation and destroyed the whole fleet. The war left us masters, therefore, not only of Manila, but of the archipelago. It was ours, therefore, by right of conquest.

I deprecated undue alarm about the difficulty of administering these distant possessions. What Great Britain had done successfully, a kindred people need not be less skilful in [doing]. No doubt it would involve material reforms in our civil service, which would be an advantage anyway. The Constitution interposed on obstacles and there would be little difficulty in so modifying our present territorial system as to adapt it to any of these islands whenever it might be thought best to relieve them from military rule. But they should be governed permanently as colonies, never with the remotest idea of permitting their admission as states in the Union.

All the talk of liberating Cubans and Filipinos offered by Spanish (mis) rule was but a grand excuse to take over from Spain.

U.S. political cartoon depicting Uncle Sam planting flags on the globe as easily as we would plant candles on a birthday cake

US options on
the Philippines

AT the conclusion of the Spanish-American War, opinion was divided in the United States over the taking of overseas territory. Naturally, the Philippines was a hotly debated issue—should we or should we not take the so-called Pearl of the Orient. President McKinley appointed a five-member peace commission to meet with Spanish counterparts in Paris and negotiate the treaty of peace. Secretary of State William Day resigned to head the commission composed of three senators, namely, Cushman K. Davis of Minnesota, William P. Frye of Maine, and George Gray of Delaware, and Whitelaw Reid, publisher of the New York Tribune.

Three out of five were in favor of expansion: Davis, Frye, and Reid. The lone anti-imperialist was Senator Gray. The chairman William Day, while appearing neutral, would not only follow the wishes of the majority but McKinley as well. That the U.S. Peace Commission would demand the Philippines from Spain was a given. In the White House briefing before the commissioners left for Paris, McKinley asked for their individual opinions regarding the thorny issue of the Philippines. According to the diary of Reid, when Frye was called on, he:

> referred particularly to the moral features of the case. [He] said that he thought that while there was some difference in New England as to the policy [of overseas expansion] and while...considerable public sentiment were opposed to any increase in territory, he thought the larger and better part of New England believed it impossible for the United States, with any show of consistency or morality, to return to the dominion of Spain territories which had once been wrested from her. He had an impression that the conscience of the religious community was going to make itself felt in this direction...On the whole, however, his talk was decidedly in favor of holding on to the whole of the Philippines, as well as to all the Spanish West Indies. He also considered the Carolines and the Ladrones important.
>
> Continuing on around the table, the President next called on Judge Day, who spoke in a strongly conservative sense against the desirability of any further territorial acquisition by the United States. He believed that with Cuba [and] Puerto Rico in the West Indies, which he thought it clear that we

would be compelled to retain, or be responsible for, we had already undertaken a very large task. He would like to get out of the Philippines with the least possible responsibility in that quarter. They were remote, had no direct relation to us, [and] would not have been thought of as a desirable acquisition but for the war; he did not see why the war had made them any more desirable.

They comprised a great multitude of islands, anywhere from six hundred to several thousand, embraced a great variety of races, pure and mixed, including many still in a state of savagery, and also a great variety of religions. A large section at the south was under the control of Mohammedans, who had never been conquered by Spain, and who were believed to be depraved, intractable, and piratical.

He thought the United States had enough on its hands now, that it had really not taken possession of this portion of the Philippines, at least, or indeed any portion excepting the harbor and bay of Manila, and second that there must be a limit to our humanitarian enterprises. Because we had done good in one place, we were not therefore compelled to rush over the whole civilized world, six thousand miles away from home, to undertake tasks of that sort among people about whom we knew nothing, and with whom we had no relation.

Judge Day's statement was given with a good deal of precision of manner, following notes which he evidently jotted down in advance, and was undoubtedly effective.

Now came the turn of Whitelaw Reid:

I dwelt upon the obvious necessity for coaling stations, spoke of the desirability of getting a point in the Carolines as well as in the Ladrones...the necessity of one island in the Carolines as a landing point for a cable stretching from San Francisco to Manila, with landing points only on United States territory.

Reid then summarized all the options presented to the president and the commission:

I spoke of the various schemes which had been presented with reference to the Philippines, mentioning the proposals: (1) that we should take only Manila; (2) that we should take only Luzon; (3) that we should divide Luzon at the peninsula in the southern part; (4) that we should turn Manila into a free city, like the cities of the Hanseatic League, guaranteeing its independence; (5) that we should take all the Philippines excepting the Mohammedan part [Mindanao]; and (6) that we should take the whole of [The Philippines].

All these discussions for nothing. While McKinley seemingly gave the peace commission room to decide, he had already made up his mind about taking the Philippines and made sure the composition of the commission had the majority on the side of annexation.

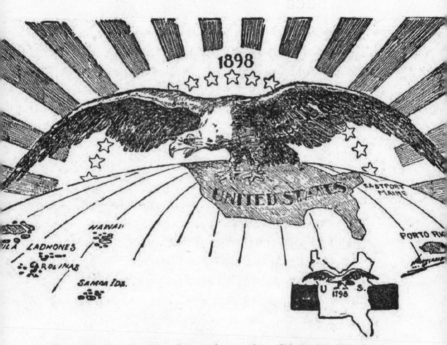

Ten thousand miles from tip to tip.—Philadelphia Press.

U.S. political cartoon that depicts the breadth of U.S. territory on a map

How the Philippines became part of US map

IF we are to believe the historical sources, the U.S. decision to take the Philippines as the "insular possession" was not made overnight. Much thought and reflection went into it. U.S. President McKinley even resorted to prayer on his knees to get divine guidance on what to do with the Philippines, which at first he could not even locate on a map.

In November 1899, as a group of Protestant clergymen stood up at the conclusion of a courtesy call on McKinley, they were asked to stay awhile longer as the president gave these thoughts on the Philippines:

> Before you go, I would like to say just a word about the Philippine business. I have been criticized a good deal about the Philippines, but don't deserve it. The truth is I didn't want the Philippines, and when they came to us, as a gift

from the gods, I did not know what to do with them.

When the Spanish war broke out, Dewey was in Hong Kong, and I ordered him to go to Manila, and he had to; because, if defeated, he had no place to refit on that side of the globe, and if the Dons [Spaniards] were victorious they would likely cross the Pacific and ravage our Oregon and California coasts. And so he had to destroy the Spanish fleet, and did it! But that was as far as I thought then. When next I realized that the Philippines had dropped into our lap, I confess I did not know what to do with them.

I sought counsel from all sides—Democrats as well as Republicans—but got little help. I thought first we would take only Manila; then Luzon; then the other islands, perhaps, also. I walked the floor of the White House night after night until midnight; and I am not ashamed to tell you, gentlemen, that I went down on my knees and prayed almighty God for light and guidance more than one night.

And one night it came to me this way—I don't know how it was but it came: (1) That we could not give them back to Spain—that would be cowardly and dishonorable; (2) That we could not turn them over to France or Germany—our commercial rivals in the Orient—that would be bad business and discreditable; (3) That we could not leave them to themselves—they were unfit for self-government—and they would soon have anarchy and misrule over there, worse than Spain's was; and (4) That there was nothing left for us to do but to take them all, and to educate the Filipinos, and uplift and civilize and Christianize them, and, by God's grace, do the very best we could by them, as our fellowmen for whom Christ also died.

And then I went to bed, and went to sleep, and slept soundly, and the next morning I sent for the chief engineer of the War Department (our mapmaker), and told him to put the Philippines on the map of the United States [pointing to a large map on the wall of his office]; and there they are, and there they will stay while I am President!

In 1898, McKinley appointed a five-man peace commission that would meet with their Spanish counterparts in Paris to negotiate the terms of peace that marked the end of the Spanish-American War. Before the commissioners left Washington for Paris on September 18, 1898, they met with McKinley. Fortunately, one of the commissioners, Whitelaw Reid, recorded the following in his diary on Friday, September 16, 1898:

Finally, the President indicated his desire to begin business and motioned us to seat about the table...he began by a reference to the [peace] protocol, and to the wide divergence of opinions that seemed to exist in the country as to unsettled questions concerning the Philippines. He said he had prepared some instructions covering the main points of our duty, but had left the final decision as to the Philippines to be filled out after the present consultation. He then asked Senator [Cushman K.] Davis to express his views.

Senator Davis said his general impression was that we certainly should retain coaling stations in the Ladrones and also in the Carolines, if that were practicable. As to the Philippines, he believed it to be a great opportunity for the United States with reference to trade in the East, as well as with reference to its naval power. He thought Manila of the utmost importance, but believed that the proper defense of Manila would require the territory back of it. He also thought that the islands adjoining would be found right and desirable, and thought it would be a mistake to abandon them.

As to the islands in the extreme southwestern portion of the archipelago occupied by Mahommedans, namely Mindanao and the Sulu group, he was not clear. He thought he should be willing to let Holland take them, as she had possessions in that neighborhood, was a friendly power, and not likely to be an unfriendly neighbor.

Publicly, McKinley was against the annexation of the Philippines. That the Philippines became an American colony proves that actions do speak louder than words.

Political cartoon that appeared on the cover of Leslie's Weekly June 1898 depicting Uncle Sam locating the Philippines on a globe

Aguinaldo trust in
US unshaken

TOWARDS the end of August 1898, the urgent telegrams sent to Aguinaldo's headquarters began to reflect the growing friction between the Filipinos and Americans. The movement of the American troops and the incursions into Filipino lines were tolerated under a cloud of great suspicion. That the Filipinos were excluded from the fall of Manila was the source of much resentment that underlined the deteriorating relations with the foreign "ally" who was soon to become an enemy.

On the morning of August 23, Pio del Pilar reported to the president: "I have received information that we should watch the Americans since they want to deceive us. Six thousand Americans have arrived and a vessel laden with ammunition. I inform you so you can be on your guard."

Before the deciphered telegram got to the desk of the president, it had to pass through Mabini. To spare

Aguinaldo from all the cables, Mabini cleared what was handed to him and sometimes gave just a summary. On Del Pilar's telegram can be found this endorsement in Mabini's handwriting:

> I have received four telegrams: two from General Pio reporting the landing of 6,000 Americans with much ammunition. He asks for rice, as the Covadonga was not able to bring any from Biñan. Montenegro reports that the pumping machines [in Marikina] have been at work since 4 p.m. yesterday, he showing the American engineers much politeness. Lt. Col. Pilar states he has given the orders to the director of the railroad concerning transportation of foreign troops without consent of the government.

Then on August 24 tragedy struck. General Riego de Dios who was governor of Cavite reported: "As a result of the occurrence an American was killed by a revolver in the hands of one of them. We shall await result of investigation. Both drunk."

Informed of the incident, the Secretary of War immediately ordered an investigation. He reported to the President: "The Governor of Cavite reports two drunken Americans have been killed by our soldiers. I tell him to have an investigation immediately and report the fact to the American commander."

By 7:00 in the evening of the same day, General Riego de Dios reported:

> Most urgent. General Anderson informs me in a letter that, *"In order to avoid the very serious misfortune of an encounter between our troops, I demand your immediate withdrawal with your guard from Cavite. One of my men has been killed and three wounded by your people. This is positive and does not admit of explanation or delay. I ask you to inform me of your decision."*

A month before, the same General Anderson has politely requested Aguinaldo for cooperation, stating that he did not wish to interfere in the affairs of Cavite, which was then in Filipino hands. After the fall of Manila, the general's tone changed. He now demanded that the Filipino governor of Cavite and his guard withdraw from Cavite!

Mabini wrote the following endorsement on the telegram.

> To Commanding General American Forces, General Merritt, from the Commanding General Philippine Forces: I have received the information of the death of one American and the wounding of three. I have been told that being drunk, they at first fired in the air, then they fought with each other. General Anderson says that said death was caused by my people, on which account I have

ordered an investigation to ascertain the truth, and to show that the Filipinos endeavor to remain in harmony with the Americans. If it should appear that any of my people are guilty, I shall impose a severe punishment.

Not satisfied with this terse reply, Aguinaldo added his own endorsement on the telegram.

Telegram received. Do not leave the post, and say you cannot abandon the city [Cavite] without my orders, and say that [enemy soldiers] was not killed by our soldiers, but by themselves since they were drunk, according to your telegram. Give up your life before abandoning that place and investigate matter.

By August 26, as a result of the Cavite incident, Filipino officers and commanders were being disarmed when they crossed enemy lines. The president received this report: "Conference with Gen. MacArthur, and he asks me to tell you that they have disarmed Spanish officers and their own not on guard, and asks that we disarm our officers and commanders who enter Manila or the American military lines, so as to avoid trouble."

Around the same time a telegram from Marikina reported: "Most urgent. I inform your excellency that the Americans are beginning to put up a telegraph line between the Deposito and Manila. I did not permit it. I await an answer."

Emilio Aguinaldo autographed this photo and provided his birth details that can be used to plot an astrological birth chart to help historians understand him more.

Mabini replied, "They can put up a telegraph line, but they cannot send troops."

Aguinaldo sent a map to the Americans describing the Filipino lines. This was delivered, and on August 30 at 5:00 in the afternoon this telegram was received from Caloocan:

> Have had conference with General Merritt. Delivered your Excellency's letter, and after describing military line that your Excellency desires, I also verbally carried out all that your Excellency directed. General Merritt replied as follows, *"Within three or four days I will send an officer to Bacoor with a map and answer to letter. I request that commanders and officers, and particularly that the president, convey to Philippine troops friendship with Americans.*
>
> *I am certain the Americans will obstruct the efforts of the people to obtain liberty and independence."*

With these reports from the field, why did Aguinaldo maintain his trust on the "alliance" with the Americans?

Americans:
From ally to enemy

MADHOUSE is the only word to describe the communications room at Bacoor on August 13, 1898. Coded telegrams from the Filipino positions outside Intramuros were flooding in, with each telegram needing to be decoded before being sent to Apolinario Mabini who then handed it to the president with a draft reply. Aguinaldo either signed the reply or added his own text to Mabini's draft, and these were encoded and sent out to the field.

A sampling of the numerous telegrams sent to Aguinaldo's headquarters in Bacoor gives us an idea of the day Manila fell to the Americans. More importantly, these telegraphic reports, though piecemeal, provide first-hand accounts of the war from a Filipino point of view.

General Artemio Ricarte at 10:22 A.M. reported:

American troops rearguard our trenches Mabolo and San Jose warn us that they will fire on us when the time comes. Impossible to remain there without disagreeing with them. Since five this morning we have been furiously attacking. Americans firing incessantly. Spaniards silent. No losses yet...

At 11:05 A.M. General Riego de Dios in Cavite reported to Aguinaldo:

Most urgent. Araneta and Buencamino having been consulted in regard to your telegram of today, they confirm capitulation, and in regard to the telegraphic note of General Anderson they are of the opinion, first, that we should continue hostilities while we ask for an explanation; second, that explanations should be in the following terms: Inquire reasons for note and ask why our troops are not to enter Manila without permission of the American commander; third, in case the capitulation is given as the reason, to answer that we do not suspend our attempt to enter Manila.

This capitulation is not favorable to our independence. General Anderson is not here. General Merritt is probably in Manila. Only Admiral Dewey is in the bay. We ask authorization to express our explanation in the proposed terms and to have a conference with Admiral Dewey in order to have our claims reach General Merritt.

The above telegram comes with the following endorsement in the handwriting of Mabini and signed by Aguinaldo:

> I authorize every assert of right, but state that we believe that we have the right to enter Manila without permission as we have a part in the surrender of the Spaniards. They would not have surrendered if our troops had not cut off their retreat to the interior. Besides, were it not for us the landing of troops would have cost them much blood. Obtain an answer as soon as possible in order to lay a protest before the consuls in case it is necessary.

Aguinaldo did not resist the landing of three contingents of enemy troops in July. He even made sure they got proper accommodations, food, and even horses. All this was forgotten in August 1898. Ricarte gives the position of his men—mostly Caviteños—as he reports to Aguinaldo at 1:30 P.M. that: "Second Noveleta, First Salinas, Fifth Malabon camped in view of Singalong. Americans wish to put us out. Give directions."

Riego de Dios reports from Cavite at 2:15 P.M. that:

> At this moment the bombardment of Manila is taking place, and we are not able to see even the shadow of an American General. In such a situation Buencamino advises to go ahead with our attack. Half an hour ago I sent Araneta to you

for a conference. [Antonio] Luna and Genato will accompany Araneta to offer their services in the trenches to advise our generals. Such is my loyal opinion.

Conflict with the enemy begins as Ricarte reports to Aguinaldo at 3:52 P.M. that:

> General Pio del Pilar informs me of the following: *"Come here, if possible, as our soldiers at the Barrio of Concepcion are not allowed to go out and we are prohibited to move any farther. We it was who succeeded in capturing the place. Come here or there will be trouble, since they are driving me away and refusing to listen to what I say."*

"I am at this very moment," Ricarte tells Aguinaldo, "going to aforesaid place."

At five in the afternoon, we hear from Ricarte again who reports:

> Colonel San Miguel here from Ermita. Regional Exposition, Agricultural College, and other buildings are ours. Our flag flies already at Ermita. Colonel Agapito Bonzo with his troops in the Perez Building, Paco. Colonels Julian Ocampo and Isidoro Tolentino are in the convent of Ermita. All houses without flag are guarded by our soldiers.

From the telegrams, it is evident that the suburbs or *arrabales* of Manila/Intramuros were in Filipino hands. From Ermita, Ricarte reports at 6:15 P.M:

> I inform you that the chiefs of our troops have reported to me that our flag at Singalong church was removed by the Americans and they hoisted theirs instead, not allowing us to approach thereto. General Pio del Pilar is at present in the barrio of Concepcion. Americans prohibited him to move any farther. How can he enter Manila?

Filipinos were effectively excluded from the surrender of Manila. And by nightfall, it had become painfully clear that the Americans transformed from "ally" to "enemy."

Spanish political cartoon depicting Aguinaldo's dream of liberty presented by Uncle Sam and his waking up to reality that Uncle Sam came with cannons to take that liberty from Aguinaldo.

Mabini strongly opposed Malolos Constitution

MABINI'S constitution was rejected by the Malolos Congress. If it was any consolation, the body likewise rejected the constitution drafted by Felipe Calderon. Failing to get either the whole or just parts of his draft constitution accepted by the Malolos Congress, Mabini wrote several letters to Aguinaldo advising him against approving the promulgation of the constitution. As a concession, however, Mabini agreed to such a promulgation provided certain amendments proposed by him are incorporated into the constitution.

From the tone of his letters and memoranda sent to Aguinaldo, it seemed that Mabini objected strongly to the empowerment of the Malolos Congress over the president. Aside from its legislative functions, the Malolos Congress also took executive and judicial powers unto itself. The diminished power of the president, in Mabini's view, was detrimental to the continuation of the civil, military, and diplomatic efforts to gain the independence of the Philippines. Concluding a letter to the president on January 14, 1899, Mabini saw other interests at work:

> If our Constitution becomes effective the Americans will be cautious about giving recognition to our cause because our desire for independence will be very evident to them.
>
> We cannot tell whether this is a political move of the annexationists, who desire our Constitution to take effect so that the Americans will lose their confidence in us and have every reason not to recognize us because we have prevented them from tampering with our Constitution.
>
> You can say that these reasonings are vague, and that they spring from my displeasure towards Congress, I leave them to you to ponder over and decide what is best to do.

Mabini worried, for example, over the power of the Malolos Congress to check Aguinaldo's appointments of department secretaries. He was concerned that although Aguinaldo was constantly assured of his veto power over laws passed by the Congress, in reality the constitution, once promulgated, would give the Congress much power. Aguinaldo could not dissolve the Congress without its consent, neither could he indict any of its representatives without its permission. Aguinaldo could not impede Congress. Mabini scrutinized the constitution and found out that whatever powers it gave Aguinaldo in one article, it neutralized or took away in another. Thus, in a letter to Aguinaldo on January 14, 1899, Mabini warned:

> In my opinion, if you approve the Constitution without the amendments, you will be contributing to the failure of our country and of our ideals. I can see it all too clearly now. That is why I find no other solution except to do one of the following:
>
> 1. Change the Representatives appointed by the Government.
>
> 2. Veto the Constitution.
>
> 3. Accept the Constitution and change the Council of Government.

Mabini ended this letter thus:

> Please do not believe in the promises of the Representatives to the effect that when the Constitution should be in force, you can do whatever you want, because what will happen will be the opposite—you shall have to do what they want. If now that we have as yet no Constitution they are already pushing you down, what will they not do when you are tied to them? May god enlighten you in these times of serious crisis.

Mabini lost out to the Malolos Congress. He was isolated from the president and eventually eased out of office. This may partly explain why in his memoirs, *La Revolución Filipina*, Mabini painted Aguinaldo in the worst possible light. Historical research teaches us not only how to read from the primary sources, but more importantly to put the sources in their proper context.

Changes in Mabini's outlook can be seen in his extant correspondence and writings. When Mabini was in the Aguinaldo Cabinet, for example, he wrote a number of letters and memoranda against Antonio Luna; but in his memoirs, Mabini turns around completely. Aguinaldo, his former boss, is painted as a villain and Luna becomes the hero. Such are the difficulties that confront historians. It is one thing to find a document and quite another to place it in context. Even rumor can be understood once it is placed in its proper context. A closer look at the intrigue and power struggles in Malolos sheds light into the wild rumors that Mabini was afflicted with syphilis.

Contrary to popular belief, Mabini opposed the Malolos
Constitution. His original draft Constitution rejected by the
Congress for another merely copied from other existing
Constitutions.

Fast-tracked Constitution

NATIONAL Artist Nick Joaquin once wrote that in the Malolos banquet "the menu is a culmination like Malolos itself, and should stand side by side with the Malolos Constitution." If Mabini were alive today he would surely take exception to Joaquin. Mabini's writings clearly show that he did not approve of either banquet or constitution. Contrary to popular belief (and to a documentary produced by the National Centennial Commission), Mabini was rabidly against the promulgation of the Malolos Constitution; however once it was in force he yielded.

According to textbook history, next to the ratification of the Declaration of Independence by the Malolos Congress on September 29, 1898, its most challenging task was to draft and promulgate a constitution that would reflect the will of the people. The deadline was rather close because Spanish and American Peace Commissioners were already in Paris discussing the disposition of the Philippines. A government and a constitution by Filipinos would complicate the Paris Peace talks.

Represented by its spokeman Felipe Calderon, the Malolos Congress held the opinion that with a constitution and a government, the Philippines was in a better position to press for formal recognition, not only from Spain and the United States but from the other world powers as well. Mabini countered that the Malolos Congress was not a constituent assembly and was not, therefore, authorized to adopt a constitution. Under the law that created it, the Malolos Congres was merely a consultative body that would propose ways to advance the revolutionary government. Mabini says it better in his own words in an undated memorandum on the constitution:

> The proclamation of the Republic presupposes a Constitution even if only analogous to those already in force in other nations. The one voted by Congress is not acceptable at this time for two reasons: first, because the constitutional guarantees it establishes to protect individual liberties cannot be upheld at present, precisely a time when the necessity of the predominance of the military element has been indicated; and, secondly, because in these difficult times it would not be convenient to establish openly the

separation of Church and the State, as it would give the supporters of the religion of the State cause to leave the Government.

Neither would it be convenient for said Constitution to govern the organization and function of the three powers. The ship of State is threatened with great dangers and terrible tempests, and the actual state of things would require, in my opinion, the advantage having, in some way, the three powers centered for the time in one hand so that it can guide the ship of State with the necessary strength and be able to elude all the perils on the way.

The "one hand" Mabini wanted to guide the "ship of State" was Emilio Aguinaldo. Naturally, behind Aguinaldo was a group of "advisers" (this sounds strangely contemporary again!), the most influential being Mabini. Not very well known is the fact that Mabini submitted a draft constitution of his own to Aguinaldo. Unfortunately, the Mabini constitution was rejected by his critics in the Malolos Congress. Felipe Calderon in his *Memorias sobre la Revolución Filipina* stated:

> Mabini had written a proposed constitution based on the Constitution of the Spanish Republic with slight variations, and, after studying it, I became convinced that it was not suitable to our

country. Pedro Paterno on his part, had given me a constitutional draft of his own which was patterned much after the Spanish Constitution of 1868. Paterno's draft, like Mabini's, proved unsatisfactory to me...I, therefore decided to write one that would be eclectic...I spent a few days studying the constitutions of other countries... Using as a basis...the constitutions of the South American republics...particularly that of Costa Rica, I prepared my own draft...One day in the drugstore of Juan Cuadra in Ermita, I wrote down the draft of the constitution, or rather had a clean copy made of the draft...

It is amazing to have one man, Felipe Calderon, single-handedly draft an entire constitution using the constitutions of other countries as cribs. The Calderon draft was then:

Submitted to the committee [in the Malolos Congress], the draft was approved with slight changes; but we encountered opposition from Mabini's partisans who wanted Mabini's own plan to be adopted...The draft having been approved by the committee, copies thereof were printed and distributed among the delegates. Thereafter, it was submitted to Congress where it was taken up in debate, from the closing days of October until November when it was approved by Congress.

How come people are made to believe that Mabini was for the Malolos Constitution? History has to be sanitized if only to hide the blemishes in what is promoted as a glorious revolution.

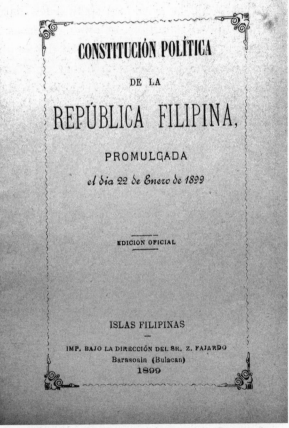

Cover of the Malolos Constitution printed in Barasoain under the direction of Z. Fajardo in 1899.

Mabini foes spread
canard on syphilis

WHEN F. Sionil Jose was writing *Po-On*, he came across rumors of Mabini's syphilis. With a novelist's eye for detail, he looked into the rumor and got confirmation from historians (one of them the late Teodoro A. Agoncillo). Thus, in the final chapters of *Po-On*, Jose weaved in the syphilis rumor. Jose creates a conversation between the village *herbolario* Istak and Mabini who, after resigning from the Aguinaldo Cabinet, had travelled to Pangasinan to rest and lick his wounds. The scene is reminiscent of the famous chat between Simoun and Padre Florentino in Rizal's *El Filibusterismo*. In both novels the nobility of one character shines as he pontificates, but in *Po-On*, the greatness of Mabini crumbles when he admits an indulgence in his youth that led to his venereal disease. In our limited experience, we can imagine people with advanced syphilis going blind or raving mad. Some people can even imagine the penitent part of the anatomy falling off, but losing the use of one's legs due to syphilis is a bit far-fetched.

A new edition of *Po-On* is out and it contains an important correction: Mabini's paralysis was caused by polio. In 1980, a team of doctors from the National Orthopedic Hospital excavated the bones of Mabini in Tanauan, Batangas, and performed an autopsy. They concluded that Mabini's paralysis that struck him when he was 31 years old was a result of polio. This information that refutes Mabini's rumored syphilis made me turn to the Malolos Congress.

Although I cannot pinpoint responsibility, I am certain that the syphilis rumor originated from the elite and mestizo-dominated Malolos Congress. On January 14, 1899, Mabini urged Aguinaldo to ignore the wealthy mestizos who had wormed their way into power through the constitution they had drafted and approved. Mabini tried his best to delay the promulgation of the constitution, and at least get some amendments in. But Felipe Buencamino threatened that Aguinaldo would lose prestige if he did not approve the constitution. Mabini countered by saying:

> Should the constitution be approved without [my proposed] amendments, no one could be appointed a Department Secretary without the approval of Congress. In my case, for example, because Congress doesn't like me, I

will be censured for anything I do until I will be forced to resign, the members will say that I am a despicable weakling who can swallow all insults. In short, no one can stay in the Department except one who knows how to regale the Representatives, do what they want, and be in cahoots with them, even to do such that will be against the interests of the country and justice. Such Department Secretaries, even if they should do badly, would be in the good graces of Congress, while the good ones would not be.

Does this sound strangely familiar? Remember how people appointed by the president to government posts today are made to wait for confirmation by the Commission on Appointments? Quotations like these make some silly people claim that Mabini is prophetic because he foresaw some of today's political problems a century ago. The words are as painfully relevant as the ones that follow. Mabini continues:

What will you do if the Secretaries you appoint be not acceptable to Congress? You will have to change them. And should new ones be neither acceptable, change them again, of course. When this happens, no right-thinking person will accept the position except the one who has an understanding with the Representatives. For this

One of the rare photos of Apolinario Mabini
standing. It was probably taken before
he was stricken by polio not syphilis as
rumored.

reason, you will yourself be forced to choose their men whether you like them or not; and since you cannot govern without a Cabinet, you will have no other choice except to please the Representatives.

Perhaps Mabini was protecting his own interest, because at one point Aguinaldo had appointed him chief justice of the Supreme Court and Congress did not confirm him since Mabini, the enemy of Congress, would become acting president in case Aguinaldo died in office. Since Aguinaldo was military president, who was often in the battlefield, the chances of Mabini taking over was rather high. Therefore, Mabini had to be blocked at all costs.

Representatives remarked that he could not become chief justice because he was lame. When Mabini heard this, he replied, "Why? Does the job entail a lot of walking?" There was more talk about his paralysis than his intellectual and academic capability for the office. In the end, the syphilis rumor came out and Mabini's moral character was undermined. To cut a long story short, intrigue eventually pushed Mabini out of the cabinet.

History hidden
in revolutionary laws

SULPICIO Guevarra's *The Laws of the First Philippine Republic* will give any interested reader a glimpse into the concerns of the Aguinaldo government. These laws and decrees reflect the challenges of the time. On August 13, 1898, a decree was issued for the regulation of prostitution. The Aguinaldo government was pragmatic enough to realize that if the world's oldest profession could not be eradicated, it should at least be regulated. This decree could have been a reaction to the increase in prostitution that resulted from the arrival of thousands of enemy soldiers from San Francisco.

Three days later, on August 16, 1898, another decree was issued disallowing cockfighting, card playing, and other forms of gambling among youngsters who should instead spend their time in athletics, such as swimming, drilling, boxing, and the like.

On the matter of health, an *Instituto de Vacunación* was created in Malolos in November 1898 to prepare various vaccines for all the provinces in the archipelago. If there was no sickness and disease in the country, would such an institute be founded? On February 17, 1899, the Philippine Women's Red Cross provided medical assistance and boosted the morale of the wounded in the Filipino-American War. There were a number of doctors and pharmacists in the Malolos government, among them General Antonio Luna, a pharmacist trained in the *Institut Pasteur* in Paris. It is not surprising to find the decree of November 2, 1898, declaring all the rules and regulations on hygiene and sanitation promulgated by the Spanish government in the Philippines to be provisionally in force.

Although the Philippine government was at war, there was still legislation for health like the following: the decree of November 5, 1898, providing for medical officers in provinces; the decree of December 13, 1898, extending the period for the filling of vacancies of medical officers in the provinces; the decree of December 25, 1898, providing for the continued enforcement of the Spanish law regarding the inspection of cattle to be slaughtered and of the fees collectible thereunder; the decree of January 25, 1899, providing regulations for the Medical Corps and for service in hospitals and in the field; and the decree of September 13, 1899, forbidding the carrying of cadavers in open coffins.

Military concerns were also addressed by the Malolos government. Aguinaldo's army was always described by the enemy in such derogatory terms as "rag tag army" because the revolutionaries were raw recruits and often lacked uniforms, shoes, and guns. When the revolutionary government was established in Malolos, steps were taken to give more dignity to the military. On November 23, 1898, a decree prescribed the form of salute to be rendered by troops, and two days later, on November 25, 1898, another decree was issued regulating army uniforms.

On February 21, 1899, a decree provided for general discipline in the army. Relations between the civil and military officials were specified in a decree dated August 29, 1899, and general orders to the army were issued in a decree of November 12, 1899. As an incentive, all males serving either in the army or the police, together with the physically disabled, hexagenarians, and town presidents, were exempted through the decree of November 11, 1898, from the payment of *cédula* tax. Social welfare was also in the agenda, as illustrated by the decrees of March 21, 1899, one providing pensions to orphans and war widows, the other abolishing compulsory labor.

Since communication was vital for government fighting a war and trying to establish itself, a number of decrees reflected this concern. On October 14, 1898, organic regulations of the communications corps were established. It seems there was also a move for the professionalization of the service, although a decree of March 2, 1899, postponed indefinitely the examinations for practical telegraphy scheduled to be given to officials of the communications corps. Telegraphic services were opened to the public following the decree of November 2, 1898, and tariffs were prescribed not only for telegrams but for mail as well. However, due to the critical situation of the times, a decree governing the transmission of telegrams had to be issued on January 20, 1899.

The history of the Philippine revolution is written from a variety of sources. One of the neglected areas are the laws and decrees of the Katipunan, the revolutionary government and the First Philippine Republic. Since laws are reactions to the challenges of the times, we can probably find history hidden in those laws and decrees.

Insurgents turned
to extortion

WHEN historical sources start to sound contemporary, it is clear proof that the Philippines and the Filipinos have not changed very much in one hundred years. Kidnap for ransom was reported in 1898 and was popularly known as "*dukut*." To make matters worse, *dukut* was done by Filipino soldiers. Extortion was hidden under false patriotism. Ransom and extortion were called "contributions" to the cause, or some sort of revolutionary tax. Then as now, affluent Chinese were the favorite and lucrative targets for *dukut*, as reported on August 27, 1898, to the president:

> Last night in the place known as Sto.Cristo the store of J. Ricafort, a Chinaman, was entered by five soldiers of our army under an unknown commander supposed to be Colonel Paua. They tried to kidnap the wife of Ricafort. At the request of P. Garcia, they desisted upon payment of 20

pesos and the agreement that 100 pesos would be paid later. If this was not done they would return to hang them. To quiet these people, I gave them a pass to assure their personal safety and exacted at the same time that they should not report this matter to the Americans...

The poor victims could not complain either to the Americans who held Manila or to Aguinaldo's government in Bacoor. What makes the above report contemporary is the threat of *dukut* and the payment of protection money on an installment plan. Teodoro Sandico, in an undated August 1898 letter to the president, made this reference to *dukut*:

The Americans have already heard of the frequent cases of kidnapping [*dukut*] occurring in Tondo, San Sebastian, and San Miguel. Last night, some of ours were surprised in the act of kidnapping a person. I have also heard that many persons are asking for contributions of war. I tell them that you know nothing of all this and that if some persons are kidnapped, it is due to the hate of the natives for the Spanish spies and secret police which is great.

It was too much trouble to kidnap Spanish spies and secret police. Wasn't it easier to assassinate them? Sandico, placed on the defensive, was already making excuses for the isolated abuses of some Filipino soldiers and officers. It must be remembered that one of the main reasons given for excluding Filipinos from the surrender of Manila was the Spanish fear that the victorious Filipinos would go on a rampage in the city to avenge the almost four centuries of colonialism. These isolated abuses, a great headache for Aguinaldo, validated Spanish and American fears.

On August 20, 1898, Mabini apologized to the president for a sloppy letter written in Spanish and Tagalog. "Excuse me for mixing in some words in Castillan," Mabini sighs, "because I have so many visitors that I cannot work in peace and my head is unquiet." The cables on his desk awaiting his endorsement prior to being forwarded to the president were not very encouraging either:

> Sr. Lopez, your adjutant, arrived and told me of many complaints regarding the behavior of the soldiers. He says that our officers carry off many horses, some of them belonging to foreigners. If the foreigners should enter a protest against such doings, I do not know what will be thought of our government.

> It is absolutely necessary that a stop should be put to the passes, and that the tax on merchandise entering Manila should no longer be exacted. It is absolutely necessary, if you think well of it, for us to promote General Pio and make him your

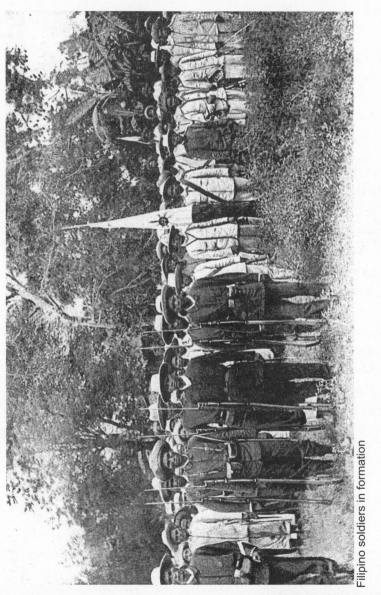

Filipino soldiers in formation

second in command. It is necessary for him to leave the vicinity of Manila, as we cannot remove him by force; and do not reprimand him.

If you approve, I will write a decree, but I reflect that nothing will succeed, if our commanders are not obliged to comply.

From the above we can see that Pio del Pilar was a force to be reckoned with, being not completely obedient to the president or to Mabini. Another telegram from the field validated the above: "Urgent. Colonel Lopez reports that our troops are still sacking and committing outrages in Malate, Paco, and Ermita, even menacing people with their arms. Urge you to take proper measures to stop the abuses."

Taxes on merchandise coming in and out of the city? This also sounds strangely familiar. Ask provincial fruit, vegetable, or fish dealers who are stopped repeatedly on the way to Manila what they go through and you will see 1898 in 1998. Is history repeating itself? Not really, we are the ones repeating history.

Education was top priority

ONE way to gauge the priorities of a government is to examine its budget. Obviously, the bigger the funds allotted for a certain branch of government, the higher its place in the list of priorities. Since the Aguinaldo government was at war, it is not surprising that the military got a big slice of the pie. Although the Aguinaldo government was besieged by an external enemy, the United States, and had to pursue a military offensive, the Malolos Congress made remarkable provisions for education.

On October 19, 1898, a decree establishing the Literary University of the Philippines was supplemented on the same day by the appointments of professors named by Aguinaldo. The Faculty of Laws and Administrative Law had Cayetano Arellano, Pedro Paterno, Arsenio Cruz-Herrera, Pablo Ocampo, Hipolito Magsalin, Tomas G. del Rosario, and Felipe Calderon; while the Faculty of Medicine and Surgery had Dr. Joaquin Gonzalez, Dr.

Trinidad H. Pardo de Tavera, Dr. Jose Albert, Dr. Salvador V. del Rosario, Dr. Ariston Bautista, Dr. Isidoro Santos, Dr. Francisco Liongson, and those with licentiates Justo Lukban and Jose Luna.

To the Faculty of Pharmacy were appointed the following: Dr. Mariano V. del Rosario and those with licentiates: Leon Ma. Guerrero (who was Rector of the University), Alejandro Albert, Enrique Perez, Manuel Zamora, and Mariano Ocampo. The star professor in the faculty of pharmacy was Dr. Antonio Luna who is better remembered as General Luna. Before he became a military man, Luna waged war on disease and germs. His battlefield was a laboratory and a microscope. Few people today know that General Luna trained in Paris at the Pasteur Institute and that he accomplished pioneering studies on malaria, water from the Pasig, and the purity of carabao milk.

If the Malolos Congress provided for tertiary education, it did not forget high school or the *segunda enseñanza*. For younger students, the Institute Burgos was established on October 24, 1898. Education in those troubled times was not contained within Malolos or Manila alone; recognition was also given to academic institutions outside the capital. On November 1, 1898, educational centers in the Ilocos were organized under a schoolmaster in the province. In other areas, the lack of qualified teachers was addressed in a decree of

November 4, 1898, that permitted public school teachers during the last days of the Spanish regime to continue in the service otherwise directed by the revolutionary government.

Despite the ongoing war, it was hoped that in areas unaffected by military operations the education of children continue. On June 7, 1899, a decree encouraged the attendance of pupils in the elementary schools established in areas under the control of the revolutionary government. One of the memorable things about children's education at the time was corporal punishment. Rizal, in his memoirs, relates the beatings he received when he studied in Biñan; Mabini, likewise, lamented the beatings he was given during his school days. It is possible that Mabini and others like him drafted the decree of February 28, 1899, forbidding the whipping of school children because it degrades the human personality.

Why was education on the list of priorities when times were abnormal and the government was engaged in a war? Most of our patriots were young men, and many were under 40, including President Aguinaldo. Many had their education interrupted by the revolution, like Emilio Jacinto who expressed his desire to continue his study of law in the Literary University in December 1898. His only problem was his close association with Andres Bonifacio. But he wrote Mabini and received

Aguinaldo's welcome to Malolos and a guarantee of his safety.

The first Philippine Republic was literally and figuratively young. An American correspondent noted and was impressed by the young men at the opening of the Malolos Congress. He wrote:

> Dark-skinned and with strong growing black hair; scarcely a sign of the frost of age showed on the head of any delegate. Few among them would have escaped notice in a crowd, for they were exceptionally alert, keen, intelligent in appearance, and as a mass, much superior to the native as one sees him in ordinary life. I will not be sure, however, that the dress was not a little responsible for the impression they made on me.

Youth was a significant factor in the Philippine revolution, which is why education was on the list of priorities of the Malolos government and the Malolos Congress.

Malolos Republic
set up tax system

THE historian who is patient and brave enough to fill in the gaps in the history of the Philippine revolution will probably conclude from his sources that necessity is indeed the mother of invention. Necessity pushed the Malolos Republic to institute a system of taxation that would address the need for revenues. The Aguinaldo government was never at peace—the Filipinos were at war first with Spain and later with the United States.

Various laws and decrees on finance give us an idea of the way the Aguinaldo government financed the revolution. The sources of income included the following: Chinese poll tax; railway and freight tax; fees collected in state courts by state representatives; rental of post-office boxes; and the sale of printed books, particularly the *Heraldo Filipino*, (the 1899 equivalent of today's *Official Gazette* that printed all laws and decrees enacted by the government).

Unclaimed property was taxed, just like the sale of useless state property and assets. There was a property tax and tax on mines, with ten percent going to the state. Then, as now, other sources of government income came from forest products; coining of money; the sale of stamped paper or adhesive draft stamps (the equivalent of today's documentary stamps); signature fees; registry and notarial fees; and even taxes and fees from labor works of prisoners.

It may come as a surprise that they also had "sin taxes" where the government derived income from the sale of lottery tickets or opium. Land and assets of religious congregations restored to the state were also taxed. Then there were the so-called contributions for war.

Tonnage dues were imposed on all merchant vessels sailing from Manila ports under the jurisdictions of the revolutionary government. Foreigners and Spaniards were allowed to engage in commerce and industry only within government territory and only on certain conditions. The regulations of the exercise of profession, commerce, or industry by foreigners in the Republic of the Philippines was later decreed on January 23, 1899. The issuance of paper money was decreed on June 30, 1899.

An export control law passed on October 6, 1899, permitted the exportation of Philippine products, except those needed in the country or that may be useful to the enemy. In far-flung places away from the seat of

Barasoain Church was the cradle of the Malolos Congress and Constitution not Malolos church that was the residence and headquarters of Aguinaldo.

government, authorization for export must first be secured from the governor or military commander of the province.

There were other taxes set up by decrees: a duty of 5% on the market value of all merchandise transported in coastwise trade, whether by rail, sea, or river (October 17, 1898); and a tax of 1% on the value of real property registered in the Registry of Property (November 7, 1898). Trademarks were regulated on January 20, 1899. The secretary of finance was authorized to regulate the sale and use of stamped documents on February 1, 1899. The form and issuance of paper money was approved in a decree of April 24, 1899, and a Bureau of Paper Money was established on June 30, 1899. On March 1, 1899, a decree providing for the method of making payments from the treasury was issued.

When one sees all these taxes, one starts to wonder if the Filipinos would soon revolt among themselves. But the government was not very harsh; sometimes it corrected itself and made concessions when it graduated taxes on government salaries.

Most intriguing was the plan for a national loan of twenty million pesos, as well as the issuance of five million pesos worth of bonds that were floated to finance the revolution. Because Mabini was very suspicious of the *ilustrados*, he tried to find the strings attached to the services and money offered to the government. Mabini warned the president about the national loan and opposed its establishment but he was overruled. The national loan and national bonds were floated, Filipinos shelled out their cash either for patriotism or for sound investment, but the funds did not seem to get to the national treasury.

In April 1899, Mabini received an anonymous letter requesting an investigation into 30,000 pesos raised in Mangatarem, Pangasinan, that seemed to have ended up in the pockets of some local opportunists. Money was given freely by Pangasinan residents who wanted to share in the financing of the revolution, but no accounting was made of the funds collected. According to the complaint, some people in town became rich overnight. It is one thing to enact laws and issue decrees for taxes and other government revenue, and another to collect money from the people—although the real problem was in remitting the funds to the government treasury. Again history begins to sound painfully contemporary.

Economics of RP revolution

ONE of the terribly neglected areas in the history of the Philippine Revolution and the First Philippine Republic is finance. We all know that Aguinaldo used the money paid for the peace bought at Biak-na-Bato in 1897 to resume the war against Spain. But that wasn't enough to buy arms, run a government, and wage war against the United States of America. Where did the Aguinaldo government get money? How was it invested? How and where was it spent?

If I were to write on the financing of the revolution, I would begin with the laws of the revolutionary government. The bulk of the extant laws of the First Philippine Republic dealt with finance, and it would be fruitful to start with the Budget Act of 1899. This act, also known as the General Appropriations Act of Provinces for the year 1899 (February 18, 1899), is very revealing as it shows us how the money of the government was distributed among the different departments and how the budget and accounting offices operated.

In February 1899, the Aguinaldo government in Malolos estimated state expenditures and came up with a total of 6,324,779.38 pesos. How this was broken down gives us an idea of their priorities. The largest piece of the pie went to the Departments of War and Navy, with the sum of 4,977,654.38 pesos. This was followed by Communications and Public Works, which had 361,366 pesos; the Treasury Department, with 354,380 pesos; and General Obligations, with 281,583 pesos. The Department of the Interior was given 203,550 pesos; Foreign Affairs, 89,040 pesos; Public Instruction or Education, 35,468 pesos; and lastly, Agriculture, Industry and Commerce, 21,688 pesos.

Because the republic was at war and the situation was "abnormal," military expense understandably took most of the budget. It is possible that in more settled times, the Department of Public Instruction, Agriculture, Industry and Commerce would get more than the military. Going through the 1899 Budget is like leafing through the annual Appropriations Act today. If you read closely (as our senators and congressmen do), you would see how the Office of the President sources funds from different places.

The War Department shouldered security expenses; the president's escort was worth 816 pesos; the Presidential Guard, 2,034 pesos; and the Pampanga Mounted Guerrillas, 1,056 pesos (these guerrillas are definitely not from Macabebe since the Americans captured Aguinaldo with Macabebe mercenaries). Closer scrutiny yielded items like the special detail or the military household of the president: one colonel (perhaps an aide-de-camp) with an allowance of 480 pesos; two lieutenant colonels at 420 pesos each; one major at 360 pesos; five captains at 550 each; four first lieutenants at 240 pesos each; and three second lieutenants at 180 pesos each.

Unfortunately, I could not trace the domestic expenses of the presidential household. How much were cooks, *lavanderas*, secretaries, etc. paid? How big was the household? How much was spent for food and what kind of food went to the president's table? Aguinaldo was allotted an allowance of 12,000 pesos. Although quite large for 1899, this amount was further augmented by "sundry expenses": salaries of servants, 1,000 pesos; light entertainment, construction of furniture, and other articles, 2,000 pesos; and ordinary expenses of the presidential palace, 3,000 pesos. "Emergency expenses" (similar to the president's contingency fund today?) was estimated at 2,000 pesos.

Since the Americans occupied Intramuros and controlled Manila Bay, the Filipinos could not collect the normal customs duties in Manila and other ports in Luzon. Thus, as for February 1899, the receipts of the government only amounted to 6,342,407 pesos which was down to thirty-six percent from that collected by the Spaniards from 1896 to 1897 and recorded at 17,474,020 pesos.

Funds were badly needed and much imagination was required to raise revenue. The much hated *cédula* torn by Bonifacio in Balintawak as a sign of defiance to Spanish rule made a comeback under the Filipino government. After Mabini reminded the president about the negative effect of keeping the *cédula*, it was abolished in principle but replaced by a "special war tax" that was supposed to be only temporary. Instead of a residence certificate, taxpayers were issued a "certificate of citizenship."

A fifty percent tax on the cost of solemn burials was imposed, as well as fees for permits to hold fiestas. One *céntimo* was levied on every pound of meat. Then, there were the usual direct taxes (city, industrial, and commercial taxes); indirect taxes from export/import duties, and fines and surtaxes imposed by Customs.

The Malolos Republic issued many laws, but these were not given time to take effect. These laws and decrees are now material for a historian who sees the unfulfilled promise of a still-born republic.

Revolution perished at Malolos meet

TO gain recognition for his government, Aguinaldo had to show that his country had all the requisites of a modern nation: executive branch, legislature, and an army. If the independence of the Republic of the Philippines could be recognized worldwide, the plans of the United States to annex the islands would be effectively countered. After all, President McKinley had assured the American people that the Spanish-American War was fought for humanitarian reasons—to liberate Cuba and not to take overseas territories.

Although Aguinaldo sent diplomatic notes and representatives to foreign nations requesting formal recognition of the Philippines as a free and independent nation, these were ignored. Representatives of Spain and the United States were in Paris threshing out the details of a peace treaty. Aguinaldo's advisers warned that the issue of the future political status of the Philippines would surely be raised, and if the revolutionary government did not have a voice in those negotiations, both Spain and the United States would decide on the Philippines as they wished. Filipinos stood to lose the independence they had recently won and fought for.

Aguinaldo's advisers pushed for the convening of the revolutionary congress, the ratification of the Declaration of Independence from Spain, and the establishment of a constitutional republic. Aguinaldo acted quickly and ordered that the delegates to a revolutionary congress convene in Malolos on September 15, 1898. By then, he had already moved the revolutionary government from Cavite to Bulacan. The assembly was to discuss the steps to be taken to secure the recognition of Philippine independence and the Republic.

Malolos was in a festive mood. Unfortunately, few people realized that this was only the calm before the storm.

Textbook history, yearly government commemoration, and the inverse of the out-of-print five-peso bill make us remember Aguinaldo standing by the window of his Kawit home during the Declaration of Philippine Independence on June 12, 1898. Nobody remembers September 29, 1898, when the Malolos Congress ratified the June 12 Declaration of Independence. It is unfortunate that in recent years much more has been written in the popular press about the Malolos banquet thrown on September 29, 1898, than about the laws enacted by the congress in its short but eventful life.

We can see from the printed invitation and the menu what the founding fathers ate for lunch on that hot September day. Some academic historians who cannot see through the food think that dwelling on the gastronomic is trivial and irrelevant. Is it? Food served that day reveals the ideology behind the Malolos Congress and the true sentiment regarding the revolution.

On top of the printed menu was a triangle with the date September 29, 1898, and on the two side panels were written—in Spanish—Liberty and Fraternity. Obviously, there is an allusion to the French Revolution. Running down the center of the menu is "*Igualdad*," but then equality was farthest from the minds of many members of the elitist Congress. The historic independence banquet was for the *ilustrados*, the government officials, military officers, and their invited guest—the *sosyal* of the time. The Malolos banquet was definitely not for the common soldier or the common *tao* who actively supported the war. These ordinary citizens, forgotten by history, were not invited to the meal that Filipinos then and even now would find difficult to swallow.

For starters, they had oysters, prawns, buttered radish, olives, Lyon sausages, sardines in tomato sauce, and Holland salmon. The main courses consisted of crab in the shell, *Vol-au-vent à la financiere*, chicken giblets *à la tagale*, mutton chops with potato straws, truffled turkey *à la manilloise*, *filet à la Châteaubriand* with green vegetables, and finally cold ham with asparagus. For dessert there were cheeses, fruits, preserves/jams, jellied strawberries and ice cream. To wash down the seven appetizers, seven courses, and assortment of four desserts, one progressed from Bordeaux, Sauterne, and Sherry, to Champagne, Chartreuse, and Cognac, and finally to coffee or tea. France was the inspiration. Our founding fathers not only took the French revolution to heart, but found French gastronomy to their taste as well.

National Artist Nick Joaquin once wrote that "the menu is a culmination like Malolos itself, and should stand side by side with the Malolos Constitution." The opposite view, however, is that the banquet was nothing more than a tasteless, unfeeling display of wealth and contrived culture in the midst of a revolution. Mabini, who strongly opposed the Malolos Constitution, writes about the architect of this Malolos fiesta, Pedro Paterno, who:

> has always distinguished himself for his love of *premature fiestas*. When he was elcted President of the Malolos Congress, he occupied himself primarily with the organization of a fiesta he labeled *popular* to celebrate Philippine Independence even if it was not yet officially recognized. We have seen that this fiesta, instead of accelerating the advent

of the independence we pine for, did not seem to do anything but frighten it away. Anyway, pursued by bad luck, Paterno's fiestas result in funerals... we know that these Paterno-inspired fiestas solemnized the decomposition of the Government and Armed Forces of the Philippines.

A historian is always confronted by the questions—what should we remember? The Malolos Congress is something to be commemorated but not glorified. Perhaps, this is why the late Teodoro A. Agoncillo entitled his landmark book *Malolos: Crisis of the Republic*. Malolos saw the death of the revolution and marked the ruin of the Aguinaldo government.

None of the delegates to the Malolos Congress left letters or memoirs describing the men and women who partook of the famous banquet whose menu has come down to historians of the late twentieth century. Fortunately, an American news correspondent, Frank Millet, gave us his, rather unflattering, view of the people at Malolos on that humid day in September 1898:

> Every man was dressed in full black costume of more or less fashionable cut, according to his means or tastes. Many of them wore full evening dress, some of them had silk hats of quaint shape and well-worn nap, others bowlers of the season of 1890, but all, to a man were in black. It was a sweltering hot day too, and they suffered for

their adherence to the etiquette of new Filipino government.

Although our biased American correspondent could not list the names of the people in attendance and could only recognize Aguinaldo, he tried to distinguish the statesmen from the politicians by their clothing. The heat was the acid test:

> But statesmen all do have to suffer in hot weather, if one may take as true the difference between a statesmen and a politician, which is that a statesmen always wears a buttoned-up black frock-coat, and a politician a sack-coat or cut-away, or any coat he likes. That difference came to mind at once when I saw these statesmen fanning themselves vigorously with their hats, just behind them the natives, politicians all of them, in cool, almost diaphanous, garments [with their shirts untucked].

Equating statesmanship in Filipinos with European clothing, he notes that if one was not in black and came in a comfortable *barong*, then one was merely a politician. Imagine wearing stuffy, heavy evening dress at a daytime event in the tropics! The only positive thing the American correspondent noted was the youth of the delegates who were described as:

> Dark-skinned and with strong growing black hair; scarcely a sign of the frost of age showed

on the head of any delegate. Few among them would have escaped notice in a crowd, for they were exceptionally alert, keen, and intelligent in appearance, and, as a mass, much superior to the native as one sees him in ordinary life. I will not be sure, however, that the dress was not a little responsible for the impression they made on me.

Was Malolos, its Congress, Constitution, and trying-hard banquet really the highlight of 1898? History textbooks tell us it is so, but a closer look reveals that Malolos was the end of the revolution.

Aguinaldo presiding over the opening of the Malolos Congress.

Aguinaldo dealt
with love, taxes

TEODORO Agoncillo used to say that it is impossible to be "objective" in history. One could be fair, but never objective. Historians confronted by various sources inevitably have to choose which to use and which to discard in writing their narrative. Selection in itself is subjective.

Anyone who goes over the five-volume compilation of documents entitled *The Philippine Insurrection Against the United States* prepared by Captain J.R.M. Taylor will be impressed by the sheer size and variety of documents presented. As Taylor's published work is in English, some researchers presume that there is no need to return to the archival documents in the original languages—mostly Spanish and Tagalog. One must visit, at least once or twice, the National Library to see that the collection once known as the Philippine Insurgent Records (PIR) and now renamed the Philippine Revolutionary Records (PRR) is so multitudinous that the documents fill the better part of a huge room. Taylor's five-volume compilation is literally the tip of the proverbial iceberg. The PRR has within it a series known as "Selected Documents" personally chosen by Captain Taylor for his five-volume work.

What was unimportant for Taylor at the turn of the century could be important for a Filipino historian in 1998, and vice-versa. When one studies the "Selected Documents" more closely, one realizes that the documents were meant to show Filipinos in the worst possible light. Isolated abuses by the Filipinos find their way into Taylor's work—but what about the abuses by the enemy troops? Surely there must have been Filipino reports about and responses to enemy abuse, vandalism, torture, rape, etc. How come these are not in Taylor? Without sweeping the truth under the rug, the Filipino historian must try to be fair if he cannot be objective.

What does the modern historian make of the "taxes" or "contributions" collected from merchants by Filipino soldiers and officers? What kind of "taxes" were imposed on produce being brought to and from Manila? Were these "taxes" legal? Did they have a schedule of tariffs and fees? It seems the receipt was a "pass" that would allow the merchant free passage through Filipino lines that surrounded the capital. General Riego de Dios, governor of Cavite, asked for instructions on August 21, 1898:

Urgent. I desire to know from Your Excellency if we should continue collecting taxes on certain incoming and outgoing articles of commerce. As the Americans object to this order, I await an answer, because we might have serious disputes between the Americans and our collectors.

Mabini drafted a reply for the president: "Until further orders suspend the collection of taxes on incoming and outgoing merchandise, port of Cavite, which Americans contend is under their jurisdiction."

On August 28, Aguinaldo was in *Cavite Viejo* (literally "Old Cavite" known today as Kawit) where he received this telegram from the colonel of the general staff in Bacoor Headquarters. Jurisdiction over tax collection was not only disputed between the Filipinos and the enemy but between Filipino commanders as well:

At this moment General Malvar's messenger has arrived bringing 15,666 in silver and 2,335 paper money. The amount has not been checked yet, as the treasurer-general has not arrived, and I do not know where he is. General Ricarte says in regard to the tax on the rice markets, that he is entitled to collect from the people of Paco, as the Spaniard did in their day. Now, Col. Tolentino has suspended it, saying that it belongs to the zone of Ermita. It would be advisable to turn over the delegate revenues of Paco under his liability,

Emilio Aguinaldo photographed in Biak-na-Bato circa 1897, the image as reproduced often crops out the photobomber in the background.

in order to avoid conflicts. That is my opinion. I, however, bow to the wishes of your excellency. No news here.

Aguinaldo had to deal not only with finances but with personal problems as well. A reprimand drafted by Mabini is to be found in Taylor's compilation. We do not know whether a final copy was sent, signed by the president but the draft alone gives us an idea of the problems Mabini had to settle before it reached Aguinaldo's desk. This reprimand is addressed to a certain Colonel Montenegro.

> A complaint has been received here against you to the effect that you have fallen in love with a woman named Pilar Leve, and that you wish to marry her in spite of her mother and against the laws in force.

> I sincerely deplore the fact that the persons in whom I have reposed my confidence abuse the same, conspiring against my authority by means of acts derogatory to the prestige of this Government... Consider that the foreign powers are at this critical moment of our history watching us, and remember that every abuse of power injures the good name of our country in a notable manner.

The woman was probably a minor and thus needed parental consent for marriage. This may seem a small and trivial matter in the context of the revolution but the complaint and Mabini's resolution show that the revolution was not just a military matter but one that involved real people and real human emotions. This is a side of history we tend to forget.